LONGMAN

CORNERSTONE
2

Anna Uhl Chamot

Jim Cummins

Sharroky Hollie

PEARSON
Longman

Longman Cornerstone 2

Pearson Education, 10 Bank Street, White Plains, NY 10606

Staff credits: The people who made up the *Longman Cornerstone* team, representing editorial, production, design, manufacturing, and marketing, are John Ade, Rhea Banker, Liz Barker, Kenna Bourke, Jeffrey Buckner, Brandon Carda, Daniel Comstock, Martina Deignan, Gina DiLillo, Nancy Flaggman, Cate Foley, Patrice Fraccio, Tracy Grenier, Zach Halper, Henry Hild, Sarah Hughes, Karen Kawaguchi, Lucille Kennedy, Ed Lamprich, Jamie Lawrence, Niki Lee, Christopher Leonowicz, Tara Maceyak, Katrinka Moore, Linda Moser, Liza Pleva, Edie Pullman, Monica Rodriguez, Tara Rose, Tania Saiz-Sousa, Chris Siley, Heather St. Clair, Loretta Steeves, and Andrew Vaccaro.

Text design and composition: The Quarasan Group, Inc.
Illustration and photo credits: See page 302.

Library of Congress Cataloging-in-Publication Data
Chamot, Anna Uhl.
    Longman cornerstone / Anna Uhl Chamot, Jim Cummins, Sharroky Hollie.
    p. cm. - - (Longman cornerstone; 2)
    Includes index.
    1. Language arts (Elementary school)—United States. 2. Language arts
(Elementary school)—Activity programs 3. English language—Study and teaching.
    I. Cummins, Jim II. Hollie, Sharroky III. Title.

ISBN-13: 978-0-13-514807-5
ISBN-10: 0-13-514807-3

PEARSON LONGMAN ON THE WEB

Pearsonlongman.com offers online resources for teachers and students. Access our Companion Websites, our online catalog, and our local offices around the world.

Visit us at **www.pearsonlongman.com**.

Printed in the United States of America

3 4 5 6 7 8 9 10–CRK–12 11 10 09

Anna Uhl Chamot is a professor of secondary education and a faculty advisor for ESL in George Washington University's Department of Teacher Preparation. She has been a researcher and teacher trainer in content-based second-language learning and language-learning strategies. She co-designed and has written extensively about the Cognitive Academic Language Learning Approach (CALLA) and spent seven years implementing the CALLA model in the Arlington Public Schools in Virginia.

Jim Cummins is the Canada Research Chair in the Department of Curriculum, Teaching, and Learning of the Ontario Institute for Studies in Education at the University of Toronto. His research focuses on literacy development in multilingual school contexts, as well as on the potential roles of technology in promoting language and literacy development. His recent publications include: *The International Handbook of English Language Teaching* (co-edited with Chris Davison) and *Literacy, Technology, and Diversity: Teaching for Success in Changing Times* (with Kristin Brown and Dennis Sayers).

Sharroky Hollie is an assistant professor in teacher education at California State University, Dominguez Hills. His expertise is in the field of professional development, African-American education, and second-language methodology. He is an urban literacy visiting professor at Webster University, St. Louis. Sharroky is the Executive Director of the Center for Culturally Responsive Teaching and Learning (CCRTL) and the co-founding director of the nationally-acclaimed Culture and Language Academy of Success (CLAS).

Consultants and Reviewers

Dear Student,

Welcome to *Longman Cornerstone*!

We wrote *Longman Cornerstone* to help you learn to read, write, and speak English. We wrote a book that will make learning English and learning to read a lot of fun.

Cornerstone includes a mix of all subjects. We have written some make-believe stories and some true stories.

As you use this program, you will build on what you already know, learn new words and new information, and take part in projects. The projects will help you improve your English skills.

Learning a language takes time, but just like learning to swim or ride a two-wheeler, it is fun!

We hope you enjoy *Longman Cornerstone* as much as we enjoyed writing it for you!

Good luck!

Anna Uhl Chamot
Jim Cummins
Sharroky Hollie

A *Cornerstone* Unit Walkthrough

Your *Cornerstone* Unit!

Cornerstones are important for building and learning.
This book will help you learn to read, write, and speak English.
Meet your book!

Kick Off Each Unit

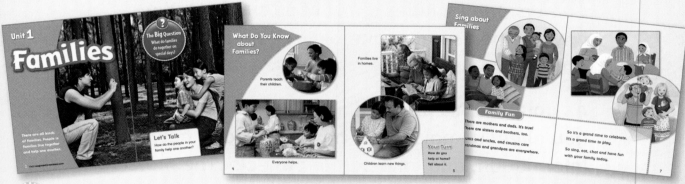

❓ Big Question
The Big Question gets you thinking about what is to come.

What Do You Know?
Talk about the unit theme.

Sing
Sing a short song to help you think about the theme.

Begin Each Reading

Vocabulary
Get to know the words *before* you read. Learn the phonics that will help you learn to read, too.

About the Story
Get a sneak peak into what the Reading is all about.

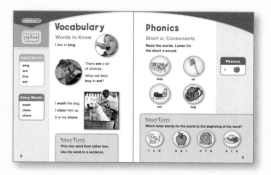

Read the Story

Readings ①, ②, and ③
Read with success!

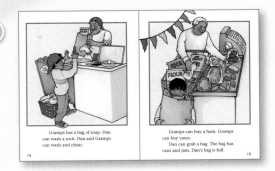

Gramps has a bag of soap. Dan can wash a sock. Dan and Gramps can wash and clean.
14

Gramps can buy a ham. Gramps can buy yams.
Dan can grab a bag. The bag has cans and jam. Dan's bag is full.
15

After Each Reading

Think It Over
Answer some questions about what you just read.

Wrap Up Each Unit

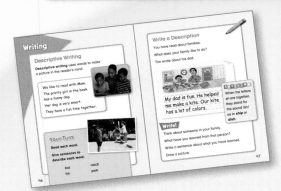

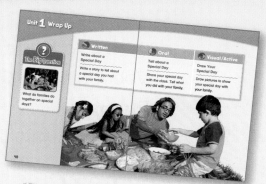

Writing
Learn about writing and practice writing on your own.

❓ Wrap Up
Discuss the Big Question with your class. Choose a project to work on and share.

Families

Unit 2
Contents

Growing Up

? The Big Question

Unit 3

Contents

What We Like

? The Big Question

Unit 4

Contents

Then and Now

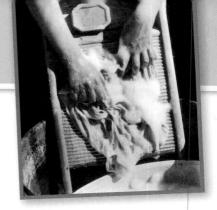

? The Big Question

Plants and Animals

? The **Big** Question

Reading I

Reading 2

Around the World

? The **Big** Question

Unit 1

Families

There are all kinds of families. People in families live together and help one another.

Let's Talk

How do the people in your family help one another?

3

What Do You Know about Families?

Parents teach their children.

Everyone helps.

Families live
in homes.

Children learn new things.

Your Turn

How do you

help at home?

Tell about it.

5

Sing about Families

Family Fun

There are mothers and dads. It's true!
There are sisters and brothers, too.

Aunts and uncles, and cousins care.
Grandmas and grandpas are everywhere.

So it's a grand time to celebrate.
It's a grand time to play.

So sing, eat, chat and have fun
with your family today.

Dan and Gramps

Sight Words

sing

are

buy

eat

Story Words

wash

clean

chore

Vocabulary

Words to Know

I like to **sing**.

There **are** a lot of choices.

What will Matt **buy** to **eat**?

I **wash** the dog.

I **clean** him up.

It is my **chore**.

Your Turn

Pick one word from either box.

Use the word in a sentence.

Phonics

Short a; Consonants

Read the words. Listen for the short _a_ sound.

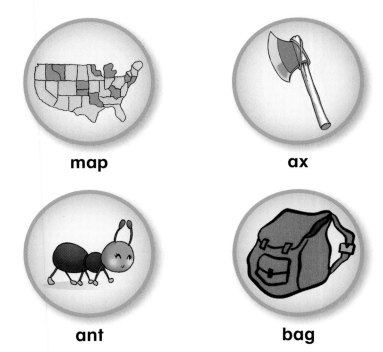

map

ax

ant

bag

Your Turn

Which letter stands for the sound at the beginning of the word?

t c d   a p l   n f h   h t a

9

About the Story

Who is in the story?

Dan

Gramps

Nan

Jan

What is the story about?

Dan and Gramps have chores to do.

Dan and Gramps

by Pam Walker

illustrated by N. Jo Tufts

11

Dan has a chore. Gramps has
a chore. Dan and Gramps can fold
the wash.

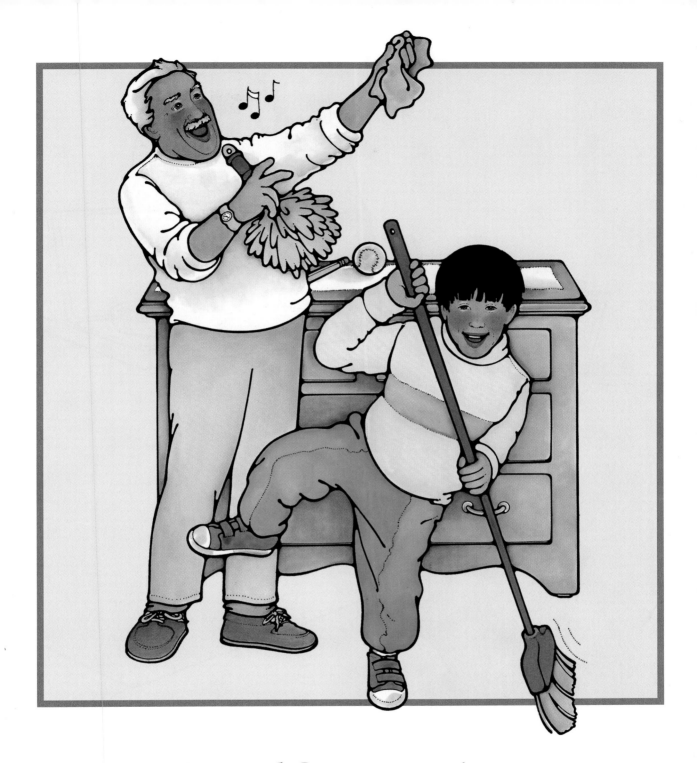

Dan and Gramps can sing.
Dan and Gramps can clean. Dan
and Gramps can sing and clean.

Gramps has a bag of soap. Dan
can wash a sock. Dan and Gramps
can wash and clean.

Gramps can buy a ham. Gramps
can buy yams.

Dan can grab a bag. The bag has
cans and jam. Dan's bag is full.

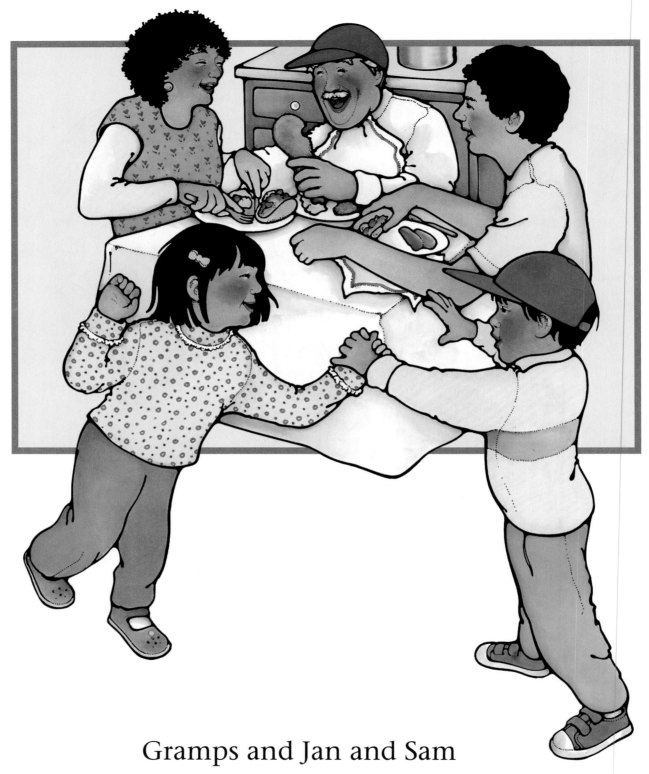

Gramps and Jan and Sam
can eat. Dan has a pal, Nan. Gramps
and Dan are glad.

Think It Over

1. Who has a chore?

2. What can Dan do?

3. What can Gramps do?

4. What can Nan and Jan do?

Grocery Stores

◀ **Samples**
This boy samples food in a grocery store.

Vegetables ▶
This family buys fresh vegetables.

Grocery Cart ▶
This family
puts things in
a grocery cart.

▲ **Labels**
This family reads
food labels.

Activity to Do!

These two pages use pictures and
words to tell about grocery stores.

- Think of another kind of store.
- Find pictures to show that store.
- Share your pictures with
  the class.

19

Children Can Learn

Vocabulary

Words to Know

I will **give** the **big** box to Dad.

It **feels** too heavy.

I do not want to get **hurt**.

Sight Words

give

big

feels

hurt

Story Words

learn

parents

children

We **learn** from Mom.

Parents teach their **children**.

Your Turn

Pick one word from either box.

Use the word in a sentence.

Phonics

Short e; th

Look at each picture. Read the word.

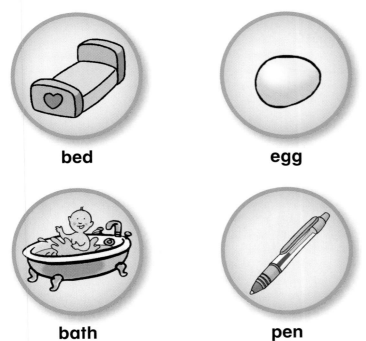

bed

egg

bath

pen

Your Turn

Which letter, or letters, stand for the missing sound?

j _ t

b _ ll

$$\begin{array}{r} 2 \\ +3 \\ \hline 5 \end{array}$$

ma _

l _ g

About the Story

What is the story about?

Parents and others help children learn.

Children Can Learn

by Dan White

Glen is a small baby. Mom and Dad help Glen. Dad can give Glen a bottle. Glen can be fed. Then Glen can get a nap.

24

Nell is not big yet. Nell is small. Nell gets help. Mom can help Nell. She can give Nell a snack.

Can Bess get milk? Yes, but Bess makes a mess. Bess feels small. Bess can ask Dad to help.

Dad can help Bess. Dad is glad
to help Bess. Bess can get milk. Bess
feels big. Bess and Dad are glad.
Bess tells Dad, "Thanks!"

Dan can learn math. Dan has a math
test. Dan gets help to pass the math test.
Dad can help Jan spell hen, pen, den,
bell, and well. Dad helps Jan spell and
pass a test.

Parents help children. Matt can get hurt. Mom helps Matt.

Matt is safe. Matt will not get hurt.

Fred has a red bat. Dad can help Fred
hit a ball. Fred can run fast.

Fred tells Dad, "Thanks." Fred is glad
Dad can help.

Think It Over

1. How does Mom help Nell?

2. What does Dan learn?

3. How does Mom help Matt?

4. Why is Fred glad Dad can help?

We Live in a Home

Sight Words

does

own

yellow

five

Story Words

house

apartment

trailer

Vocabulary

Words to Know

Does Mel **own** a **yellow** house?

Five people live in Mel's house.

Tina lives in a **house**.

Jed lives in a big **apartment**.

We live in a long **trailer**.

Your Turn

Pick one word from either box.

Use the word in a sentence.

Phonics

Short i; sh

Look at each picture. Read the word.

dig

ship

ill

ink

Phonics

i

sh

Your Turn

Which letter, or letters, stand for the missing sound?

l __ ps

sw __ m

fi __

p __ g

33

About the Story

Who are some people in the story?

Ned and Dad

Jen, Jim, and Mom

What is the story about?

People live in different kinds of homes.

We Live in a Home

by Nan Capman
illustrated by Elliot Kreloff

Get up! Get out of bed! Tell us where
you live. Let us see!

Jen and Jim live in an apartment. It has steps.

Jen wants a big pet. The pet will not fit. Jim wants a fish. The fish can fit in a bowl. Mom does not want a pet.

Ted and Tam live in a yellow trailer.
Ted and Tam have a pet. The pet is a
black cat. The black cat is Bill. Ted and
Tam think Bill is the best cat.

Your Turn

Work with a partner.
Take turns.

Read the passage:

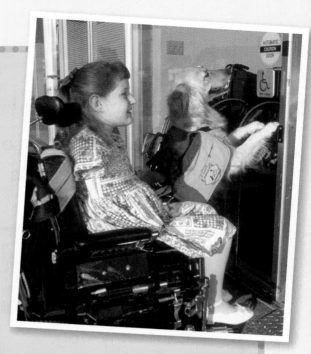

I took my puppy for a walk to town. We saw lots of shops. I wanted to buy a pencil for me and some ribbon for my mom. I saw a yellow candle that was very pretty. I bought the candle. I will get the pencil and the ribbon the next time I go to the store.

- Which words have 2 syllables?
- How do you know?
- List the words in your notebook.

Writing

Descriptive Writing

Descriptive writing uses words to make a picture in the reader's mind.

We like to read with Mom.

The pretty girl in the book has a funny dog.

Her dog is very smart.

They have a fun time together.

Your Turn

Describe the picture.
Make up sentences.
Use these words.

bat   catch

hit   park

Write a Description

You have read about families.

What does your family like to do?

Tim wrote about his dad.

My dad is fun. He helped me make a kite. Our kite has a lot of colors.

Write!

Think about someone in your family.

What have you learned from that person?

Write a sentence about what you have learned.

Draw a picture.

Unit **1** Wrap Up

The **Big** Question

What do families do together on special days?

✎ Written

Write about a Special Day

Write a story to tell about a special day you had with your family.

Oral

Tell about a Special Day

Share your special day with the class. Tell what you did with your family.

Visual/Active

Draw Your Special Day

Draw pictures to show your special day with your family.

Unit 2
Growing Up

All living things grow. All things change as they grow.

The Big Question
What do you want to be when you grow up?

Let's Talk

Tell about how you have changed since you were a baby.

51

What Do You Know about Growing Up?

Living things grow up.

A bear cub grows up to be a big bear.

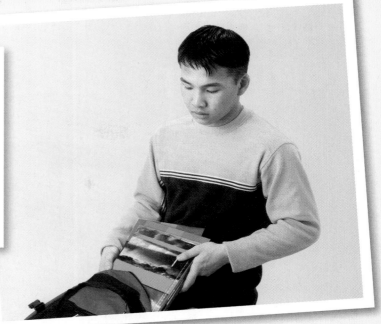

A baby grows up
to be a teenager.

A seed grows
to be a flower.

Your Turn

Think of how
you will grow up.
Tell about it.

Sing about Growing Up

Growing Up

We all grow up, and we all change.

We grow to boys and girls.

We learn new things as we grow

And help each other more.

Spot Is a Pal

by Tracey Baptiste

illustrated by Elizabeth Allen

59

This is Spot. I was five when I
got Spot. Spot was light, and I could
hold him. Did my puppy eat a lot?
Yes, Spot did.

A year has passed. Now Spot is
not as small. Spot got big. Spot and I
played a lot. We ran and ran and ran.
Spot and I had fun. Did Spot eat a lot?
Yes, Spot did.

Spot and I got big, and I turned six. I had a cake and a hat. I got gifts from Mom and Dad. Spot sat with me. Spot is a funny pet.

Spot and I sit and grin. Now I cannot hold Spot. Spot is not as light. Spot and I play and learn tricks. Spot can do a lot of tricks. Spot can sit, stop, and beg.

Spot is a funny pet. I got a lick from Spot as a kiss. Spot is my best pal.

Another year has passed. Spot is a grown-up dog. I am not grown yet. I am still a kid. I will be a big kid when I am ten. I can't wait to be a big kid. Spot will still be my best pal.

Think It Over

1. Who is Spot?

2. How old are Spot and the boy?

3. What do Spot and the boy do together?

4. How has Spot changed by the end of the story?

Kud and Husk

Vocabulary

Words to Know

It is cold, **but** I **play** outside.

I use a **coat for** warmth.

When it's very **cold**, water turns into **ice**.

Rain turns into **snow**.

Sight Words

but

play

coat

for

Story Words

cold

ice

snow

Your Turn

Pick one word from either box.

Use the word in a sentence.

Phonics

Short u; ch

Read the words. Listen for the short *u* sound.

up

lunch

sun

hug

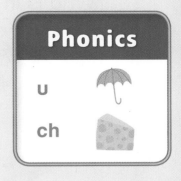
Your Turn

Which letter, or letters, stand for the missing sound?

b __ s

__ ick

t __ b

dr __ m

About the Play

Who is in the play?

Kud

Mom

Husk

What is the play about?

The play is about a boy who gets a new coat.

Kud and Husk

by Cara Church

illustrated by Diana Kizlauskas

Mom: Kud, the sun is not up now. It is dusk. It is damp and cold.

Kud: Yes, it is a bit damp, and I am chilled. But Husk will help me keep warm. I will get my coat and put it on.

Husk: Ruff, ruff, ruff.

(*Mom and Kud went in the hut*)

Mom: I have a coat in this bag.
I bet it will fit you.

Kud: Let me see it. Is it a coat that is
for me? Will I fit in it?

Husk: Ruff, ruff, ruff.

Mom: It will fit. I will fix it for you. I will fix it so it will fit. I will fix it so you will not get cold.

Kud: I like it. Husk and I can play in the snow and ice. It will be such fun.

Husk: Ruff, ruff, ruff, ruff, ruff.

Think It Over

1. Who are the characters in this play?

2. What problem does Kud have?

3. How does his mom help him?

4. What do Kud and Husk want to do?

The Ugly Duckling

Vocabulary

Words to Know

Were these kids ever babies?

Now they can walk.

By next year, they will skip **or** run!

People like to watch these **beautiful swans**.

Sight Words

were

now

by

or

Story Words

people

beautiful

swans

Your Turn

Pick two words from the bottom box.

Point to pictures that show those words.

Phonics

Long a

Read the words. Listen for the long *a* sound.

cake

bake

Phonics

a

snake

plate

Your Turn

Which word names the picture?

Tell if the word has a long *a* sound.

lake   lock

wave   wake

chick   check

whale   wade

About the Poem

What is the poem about?

This poem is about a duckling that grows up to be a swan.

Where does the poem take place?

The poem takes place in a bird's nest and in water.

The Ugly Duckling

by Molly Matt
illustrated by Helen Cann

A big duck sits in a nest by the lake.
A nest with blades of grass is safe.
One big egg! Is it real or is it fake?

This big egg will crack, crack, crack.
First, the chick will peck, peck, peck.
Then, it will go quack, quack, quack.

Mom Duck and chicks take a trip up a lane.
Ducks make fun of him and hiss.
It makes him sad – he is not the same.

As he swims by, ducks call him names.
A frog tells Duck to just be strong.
But it makes him sad he can't play games.

Now it is winter, and Duck is still sad.

Big flakes drop and stick as he sits on a lake.

If he were the same, this duck would be glad.

Then came the day Duck bent his
long thin neck. "I am a beautiful white
swan, no less!"

He was so glad he almost wept.

People stop and stand and wave.
Duck is glad he is not the same.
That little glum duck is now big and brave.

Think It Over

1. Who is the main character of this poem?

2. Why is he sad?

3. Who is a friend to the duckling?

4. What happens at the end of the poem?

Fairy Tales

Wolf ▶

Little Red Riding Hood meets the wolf in her grandmother's house.

◀ **Tower**

Rapunzel lives in a tower and has long golden hair.

86

Stalk ▶

Jack gets beans that grow into a big stalk.

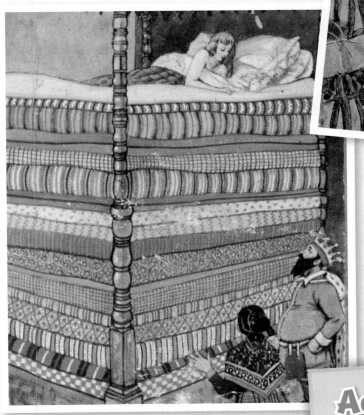

▲ **Mattress**

This princess can feel something as tiny as a pea under many mattresses.

Activity to Do!

These two pages use pictures and words to tell fairy tales.

- Think of another fairy tale.
- Make pictures to show what happens in that fairy tale.
- Share your pictures with the class.

87

Word Analysis

Compound Words

The word **campfire** is a **compound** word. It is made up of two smaller words, **camp** and **fire**.

cupcake	bedtime	sunrise
cup + cake	bed + time	sun + rise

Look for smaller words in larger words to help you say the larger words.

Rule Box

Look for the smaller words that make up compound words. This will help you find the meanings of the larger words.

back + pack = backpack

A **backpack** is a bag carried on your back.

Your Turn

Work with a partner. Take turns.

- Read each word below.

- Look for the smaller words in each compound word to help you say the word.

- Tell what the word means.

1. bookmark
2. lunchroom
3. rainbow
4. sunflower
5. homework
6. jellyfish

Writing

Persuasive Writing

You can write to persuade someone about something. Imagine you want to persuade your parents to let you take karate lessons.
You have to give good reasons!

I want karate lessons.

Karate lessons will make me stronger. I will make new friends.

Your Turn

Read each sentence. Which sentence is persuasive?

1. I like summer camp.

2. In camp I will learn many things.

3. My best friend is going to camp.

4. It is sunny at camp.

Write a Persuasive Story

John wrote a persuasive story about what he wants for his birthday.

I would like a bike for my birthday. Riding a bike is good exercise. It is fun to be outside in the fresh air. I will be very safe when I ride.

SPELLING

Look for smaller words to help you spell other words.

sun + light = sunlight

Write!

Think about something you really want.

Write about it. Remember to give good reasons.

The Big Question

What do you want to be when you grow up?

Written

Write about Growing Up

How will you have changed when you grow up? What will you have learned? Write about it.

Oral

Talk about Growing Up

Tell the class about what you want to be when you grow up. Why do you want to be that?

Visual/Active

Draw Yourself as a Grown Up

Draw pictures that show how you will look when you grow up.

Unit 3

What We Like

Some people like some things. Some people like other things. People's likes can be very different!

Let's Talk

Tell about things and activities you like to do at home, at school, and with your friends.

95

What Do You Know about What Children Like?

Some children like fruit.

Some children like to play outside, even when it's very cold.

Some children like to help.

Some children like sushi!

Some children like big snakes.

Your Turn

Name three

things you like.

Tell about them.

97

Sing about What We Like

What We Like

What we like you may not like,

ee-i-ee-i-o.

And what you like we may not like,

ee-i-ee-i-o.

I like birds and I like dogs,

ee-i-ee-i-o.

And you like pigs and you like cows,

ee-i-ee-i-o.

With a woof, woof here,

And a tweet, tweet there,

Here a moo, there an oink,

Everywhere a moo, oink.

What we like you may not like,

ee-i-ee-i-o.

A Special Time

Words to Know

My birthday is a **special day**.

I **laugh** with my **family**.

Today we had fun at the **beach**.

We all played **baseball**.

Then we climbed a **tree**.

Sight Words

special

day

laugh

family

Story Words

beach

baseball

tree

Your Turn

Pick one word from either box.

Use the word in a sentence.

Phonics

Long i

Read the words. Listen for the long *i* sound.

time

kite

nine

slide

Your Turn

Point to the word that names the picture. Read the word.

white   wet

file   five

smell   smile

pig   pipe

About the Story

Who is in the story?

Mr. Grimes

Jed

Sam

Tim

Tam

Len

What is the story about?

The story is about fun times in families.

A Special Time

by Pam Walker

This is Mr. Grimes and his family. It is a special time. Mr. Grimes likes to eat and have fun with his family. Everyone laughs and has a fine time.

Jed and his family like to eat outside
by the lake. Jed smiles and takes a big bite.
It is a special time.

Sam's dad takes him to a baseball game.
The game is a special time. They sit in
the red seats. Dad and Sam can see it all
from there!

Sam and his dad eat snacks. Sam jumps up to get a ball. It is a special time. Sam and his dad have a lot of fun.

Tim's mom and dad take him and his
sister Val on a beach trip. It is a special time.
Val and Mom don't like to dig in the
sand. Val and Mom like to walk on the sand.
Waves crash behind them. It is a fine time.

Tam and her mom like to have fun on
the swing. Tam and Mom swing and swing.
It is a special time. Tam sings a fun song.
Mom and Tam swing and clap to a fun song.

Len and his dad like to hike. They hike one mile. Then they take a quick rest by a big tree. Dad tells Len a tale that makes him smile and laugh. It is a special time.

Think It Over

1. What does Mr. Grimes do with his family?

2. What do Sam and his dad do at the game?

3. How do Tam and her mom have a special time?

4. What do Len and his dad do after the hike?

Who Woke Up?

Vocabulary

Words to Know

Sight Words

who
keep
some
cold

Story Words

roost
beehive
horse

Who planted these flowers?

I will **keep some** of them.

Flowers do not like **cold** weather.

A bird likes to **roost**, or rest.

Bees live in a **beehive**.

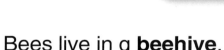

My favorite animal is a **horse**!

Your Turn

Pick one word from either box.

Use the word in a sentence.

Phonics

Long o

Read the words. Listen for the long *o* sound.

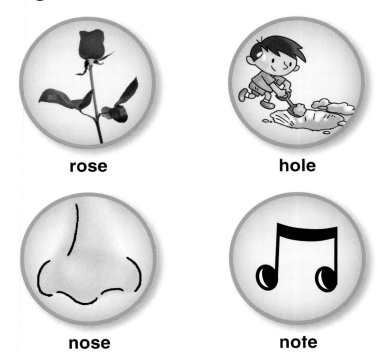

rose

hole

nose

note

Your Turn

Point to the word that names the picture. Read the word.

rope   rip

pot   pole

bun   bone

hill   hole

About the Story

Who is in the story?

Bob

Mike and Jim

Kate

Jane

Jan

kids

Where does the story happen?

The story happens indoors.

The story happens outdoors.

Who Woke Up?

by Carrie Poole

illustrated by Christine Schneider

Bob woke up. The sun came up, too. The
hens like to roost in nests. Bob woke up a hen
and got an egg. Bob can get lots of eggs. Bob
will keep some eggs. Bob will sell some eggs.

Cam and Ron and Sal like to pet Rose on her soft nose. Jan is glad that Rose gives them a big smile.

Dan and Nan and Rob and Pam woke
up. The kids have cold milk and a snack.
Dan tells a joke. Nan and Rob and Pam
can laugh and have a good time.

Think It Over

1. What did Bob get from the hen's nest?

2. What do Mike and Jim eat?

3. Who gets milk from Bell?

4. Who is Rose?

Vocabulary

Words to Know

When **we** are **done** with practice, we rest.

Sight Words

we

done

ball

down

I hold the **ball** up and then drop it **down**.

I like to kick the **football**.

Story Words

football

soccer

middle

My friend Sarah plays **soccer**. She is in the **middle**.

Your Turn

Pick one word from either box.

Use the word in a sentence.

124

Phonics

Long u

Read the words. Listen for the long *u* sound.

cube

cute

use

Your Turn

Name the pictures.

Which words have the same sound as the *u* in *tube*?

About the Story

What is the poem about?

The poem is about playing with different kinds of balls.

Playing Games

by Stacey Hill

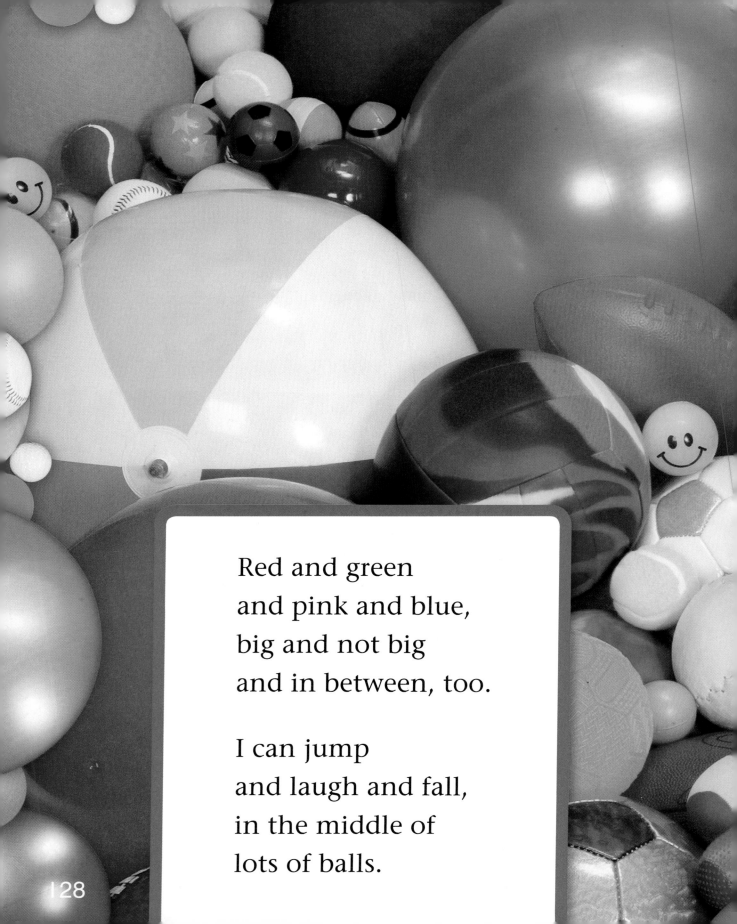

Red and green
and pink and blue,
big and not big
and in between, too.

I can jump
and laugh and fall,
in the middle of
lots of balls.

Up I jump
and down I drop.
I sing a tune.
I will not stop.

Up I pop.
Here I am!
This is me.
I am Sam!

129

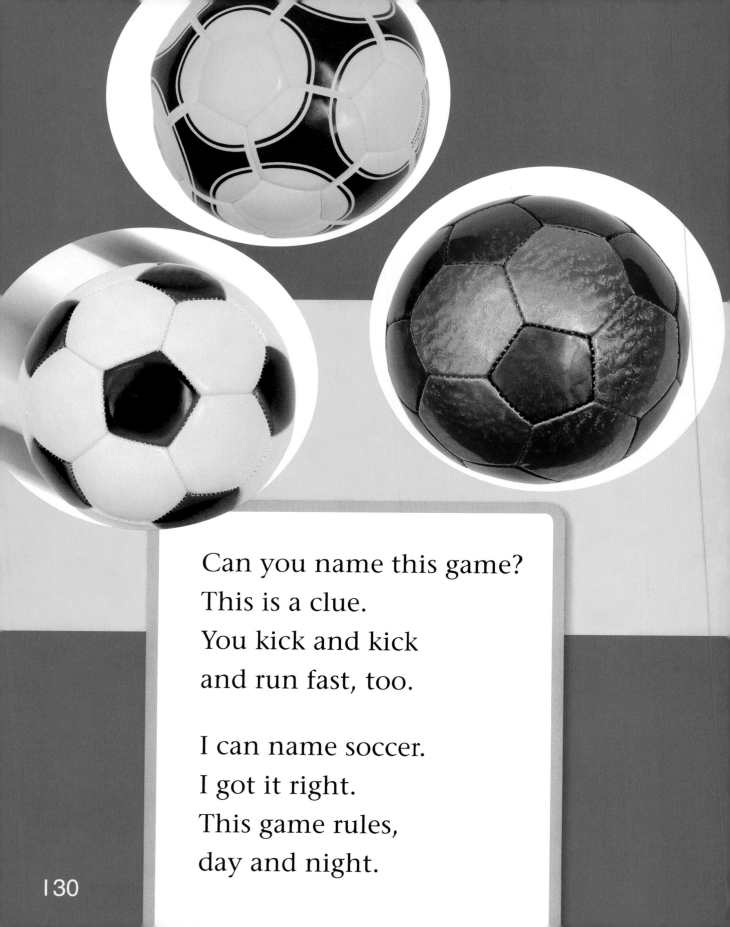

Can you name this game?
This is a clue.
You kick and kick
and run fast, too.

I can name soccer.
I got it right.
This game rules,
day and night.

I like to play soccer.
It is a fun game.
We kick and block.
I am glad you came.

In this game,
we run and run.
I am so tired
when a game is done.

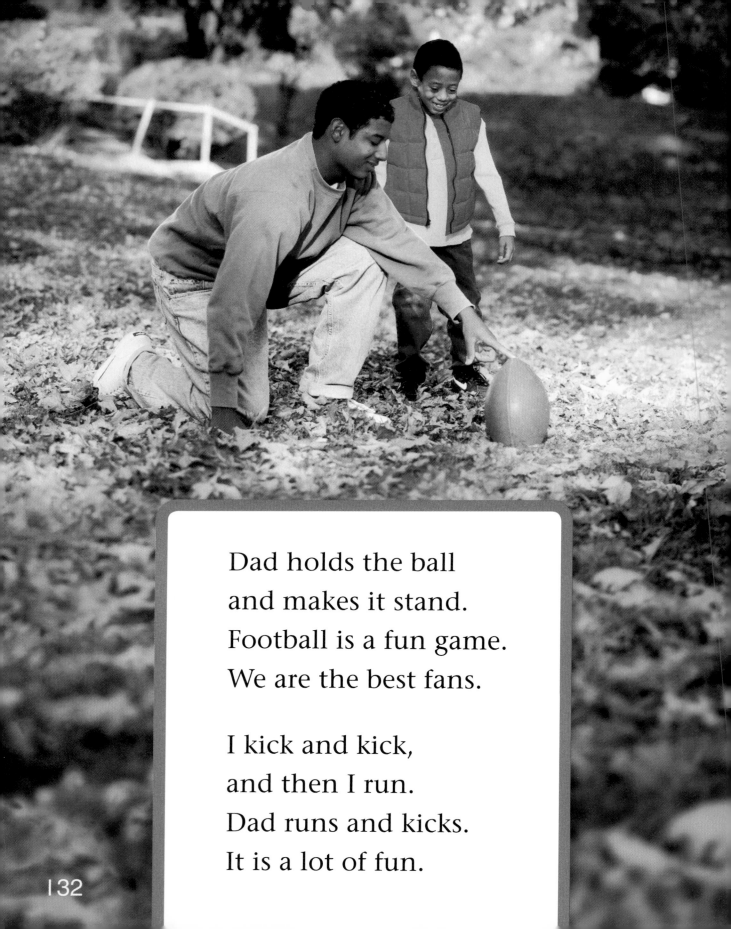

Dad holds the ball
and makes it stand.
Football is a fun game.
We are the best fans.

I kick and kick,
and then I run.
Dad runs and kicks.
It is a lot of fun.

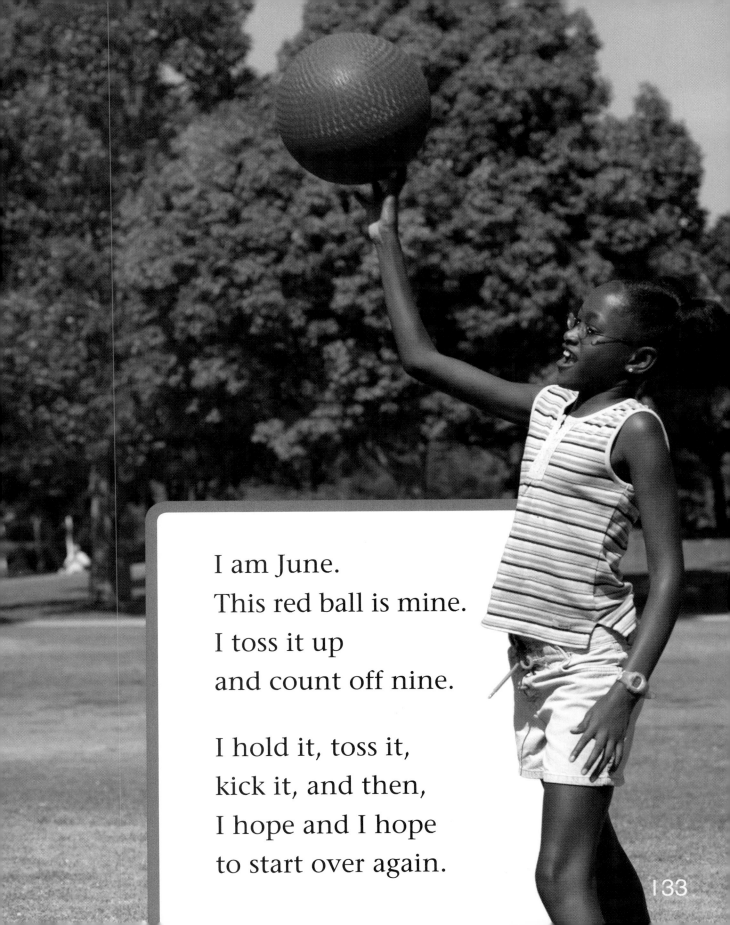

I am June.
This red ball is mine.
I toss it up
and count off nine.

I hold it, toss it,
kick it, and then,
I hope and I hope
to start over again.

133

My name is Sue.
This game is fun.
We play 18 holes,
and I am done.

I use a club
And tap it softly.
Will it go in?
My nice dad helps me.

Think It Over

1. What does Sam like to do?

2. What do you do when you play soccer?

3. What does Dad do with the football?

4. What game does Sue play?

Playing Ball

Teams

Football is a sport that needs two teams to play a game. ▶

Hoop

◀ In basketball, the ball must go through a hoop.

Bowling

The bowling ball knocks down pins at the end of the lane. ▶

Baseball

▲ There are nine players on a baseball team.

Activity to Do!

These two pages used words and pictures to tell about different balls.

- Think of another game or sport that uses balls.
- Find pictures to show how the balls are used.
- Share your pictures with the class.

Antonyms and Synonyms

Antonyms are words that mean the opposite.
Synonyms are words that mean the same.

Antonyms	Synonyms
cold ⟶ hot	jump ⟶ hop
in ⟶ out	big ⟶ large

Antonyms

It is **cold** in winter.
It is **hot** in summer.

Synonyms

I go to a **big** school.
I go to a **large** school.

Your Turn

Work with a partner.
Take turns.

- Read each sentence below.

- Replace the underlined words with a synonym or antonym from the box.

big	now	warm	jacket

1. I like to play with my <u>little</u> brother.

2. It was so <u>hot</u>, I stopped running.

3. Where did you find my <u>coat</u>?

4. May we please talk <u>later</u>?

Writing

Expository Writing

Sometimes, authors explain things from real life. This kind of writing is called **expository writing**.

Soccer uses a round ball.

Eleven players are on a soccer team.

A team wins by scoring more goals.

Your Turn

Look at the picture.

Which sentence explains things about the picture?

1. Most people are good players.
2. Tennis is easy!
3. To play tennis you need a racket and a tennis ball.
4. I want to take tennis lessons.

Write an Expository Paragraph

Jan wrote an expository paragraph about the game of tennis.

I like to play tennis. You need a racket and a ball. You have to run fast. You hit the ball over the net to the other person.

SPELLING

Change *-y* to *-ies* to make some plurals.

party ⟶ parties

Write!

Think about your favorite hobby or sport. Write about it. Explain what it is and what is done.

141

Unit 3 Wrap Up

The Big Question

What things do
you like?

Written

Write about a Favorite Outdoor Place

Where is it? What does it
look like? Why do you like
to go there?

Oral

 Visual/Active

Retell a Favorite Story

You probably know many stories and have read many books. Retell the story you like best.

Draw a Favorite Activity

Draw a picture of an activity you like to do. Share your picture with a friend.

Unit 4

Then and Now

Things are different now than in the past. We learn new things every day.

The **Big** Question

How is life today different than it was a long time ago?

Let's Talk

Talk about the changes in your community. What things are new? Are they different than before?

What Do You Know about Then and Now?

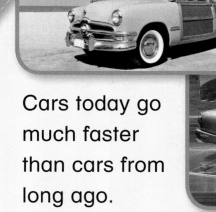

Cars today go much faster than cars from long ago.

In the past, people wrote hand-written letters to their friends. How do you write letters to your friends?

One of the games children used to play was horseshoes. What games do you like to play now?

In the past, it took a long time to travel by horse and buggy. How do you travel now?

Long ago, the best way to cook food was on a stove. How else can you cook food today?

Your Turn

If you were born before there were cars, what would you do for fun? Tell about it.

147

Sing about Then and Now

Then and Now

My grandma didn't have e-mail.

She didn't have a computer.

She just wrote letters to all of her friends

and popped them in a mailbox.

Things have changed a lot since then.

We have many inventions.

Things will change again someday,

and pop we're in the future.

Times Change

Vocabulary

Words to Know

My **friends** and I cross two **roads** on our way to school.

My dad is **very** helpful. He shows me how to write a **letter**.

Sight Words

friends

roads

very

letter

It is **simple** to write an **e-mail** to our friend.

Story Words

simple

e-mail

board

Long ago, children wrote on a **board** at school. They still do.

Your Turn

Pick one word from either box.

Use the word in a sentence.

Phonics

Long a; ch, th

Look at each picture. Read the word.

pail

chick

thick   thin

spray

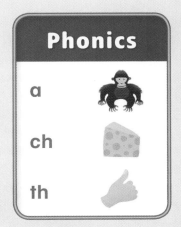
Your Turn

Point to the word that names the picture. Read the word.

gray   grape

rain   rave

snail   snap

chain   cloth

About the Story

What is this story about?

**The story is about
the past.**

It is also about the present.

Times Change

by Blaze Molloy

A long time ago, we drove on roads that had a lot of rocks and bumps. A horse led the way. We used a stick and a rope to tell him which way to go. The rope got pulled to say, "Stop!"

We drive on safe, paved roads today. We can get home fast when we drive.

An airplane can go very fast. We can pass time on a long plane trip. Sing a long song. Play a fun game. Take a quick nap. Wake up in Spain!

This mom and dad and kids play
a game named checkers. It is a simple
game with just a board and game pieces.
This mom and dad and kids play to win.

A bunch of kids play this game. It has bells that ring and lights that shine. The kids use electricity to play this game. A plug goes in the wall. Kids play this game to win!

This lady used a pen to write a letter. Next, she put a stamp on it. Then, she put it in the mail.

We can still use stamps, but now we can send e-mails. A letter may take days to get to a friend. An e-mail is fast. It takes less than a day to get an e-mail to a friend.

Think It Over

1. How did people travel in the past?

2. What is checkers?

3. What do some games need to work today?

4. What can we use today to contact a friend?

Changing Times

Locomotive ▶
These people are riding on a steam locomotive from 1845.

▲ Passengers
This is a bullet train in Japan. It carries passengers at very high speeds.

Television ▶

This family from the 1950s gathers around their black and white television.

▲ **Popular**

Wide-screen televisions are popular today.

Activity to Do!

These two pages use words and pictures to tell about how times change.

- Think of another invention that has changed the way people live.
- Find pictures of this invention.
- Share your pictures with the class.

Vocabulary

Words to Know

Long **ago,** people put clothes on a line to **dry.** **Today** people use clothes dryers.

Sight Words

ago

dry

today

In the past, people used a **washboard** to wash their clothes. Today, people use a washing **machine.**

Story Words

washboard

machine

baby

This **baby** sits in a laundry basket.

Your Turn

Pick one word from either box.

Use the word in a sentence.

Phonics

Long e

Look at each picture. Read the word.

tree

feet

read

me

Phonics	
e	

Your Turn

Point to the word that names the picture. Read the word.

sheep   ship

beach   back

green   grin

mat   meat

About the Story

What is in the story?

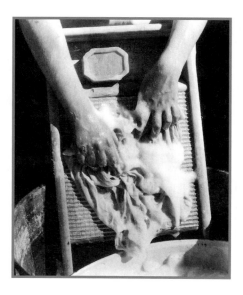

**There is
a washboard.**

**There is a
washing machine.**

Clean Clothes

by Eri Majima

It is time to clean your clothes. How do clothes get clean today?

How did clothes get clean a long time ago? You needed a stream, a washboard, soap, and strong hands. Scrub! Scrub! Scrub! Scrub! Scrub!

Dip! Scrub! Dip! Scrub! Dip! Scrub! Dip! Scrub! Get the clothes clean and fresh. A long time ago, this washboard was a way to get clothes clean.

This man scrubs and scrubs in a tub while his baby plays. He may get tired. He may want to quit. But if he doesn't clean his clothes, his family will wear clothes filled with dirt and grime.

Fresh, clean clothes hang on the line.
Pins hold the clothes up so they will
stay on the line. The sun shines on the
wet clothes. The sun will heat up and
dry the clothes.

In the past, it was a big job to
clean clothes. It took a lot of time to
keep a family in fresh clean clothes.
That was then.

And this is now.

Today we use a big machine. We put clothes and soap in it. We close the lid and set the time. Then we wait for clean, fresh clothes. We cannot put them on yet. They are still wet.

The wet clothes will need to dry. Set the time and wait a while. Sweep the deck. Read a book. Take a nap. Then fold your soft, clean clothes. Put them in neat piles. It feels fine to put on clean clothes with a sweet, fresh smell.

Think It Over

1. How did people wash clothes in the past?

2. What is a washboard?

3. How do people wash clothes today?

4. What can you do while your clothes are drying?

Ice Cream Cones

Vocabulary

Words to Know

The ice cream truck is **near** where we live.

Chocolate **sure** tastes **good**. How many **other** flavors are there?

Sight Words

near
sure
good
other

Story Words

tasty
treat
waffle

Ice cream is a **tasty treat!**

I love ice cream in a **waffle** cone.

Your Turn

Pick one word from either box.

Use the word in a sentence.

Phonics

Long i; soft g

Look at each picture. Read the word.

sky

child

light

stage

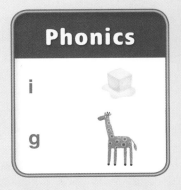

Phonics

i

g

Your Turn

Point to the word that names the picture. Read the word.

page   pig

cry   crime

file   fly

note   night

About the Story

What is the story about?

The story is about ice cream.

Ice Cream Cones

by James Dubois
illustrated by Stephen Snider

177

Ice cream is a tasty treat. We can sit in an ice cream shop on a hot night and eat this treat. Do you like to eat ice cream?

Today, we eat ice cream in cones. But in the past, ice cream came in a dish.

A big fair was held in 1904. The sun was bright and high in the clear, blue sky. A lot of kids and adults came to play and have fun. They were hot. They ate a lot of ice cream.

An ice cream man put a scoop of ice cream in each dish. The ice cream tasted good. A lot of people ate it. The ice cream man ran out of dishes. But he had a lot of ice cream left to sell. He was not sure he could sell it all. The ice cream might melt if it didn't sell.

A waffle man was nearby. He came to help. He made a cone shape. Then the ice cream man put a scoop of ice cream in the cone. These men had made an ice cream cone!

Folks liked to eat ice cream cones at the fair. They held ice cream cones in their hands. Ice cream cones were fun to eat. The kids and adults did not have to give a dish back to the ice cream man. Ice cream sure got easy to eat.

Kids ate ice cream cones with each other. Kids sat on a step and ate ice cream cones. They picked the kind they liked best. Kids ate it up, and it tasted great. It is a treat a lot of kids like better than any other treat.

Kids still buy a lot of ice cream cones. Kids get ice cream cones from a truck. The trucks drive near kids' homes. When the trucks stop, kids line up for ice cream.

Kids still eat this treat on a hot day. It still tastes good!

Think It Over

1. How did people eat ice cream in the past?

2. How do most people eat ice cream today?

3. What happened to the ice cream man's dishes?

4. Where can children buy ice cream today?

Multiple-Meaning Words

A **multiple-meaning** word has more than one meaning.

The word *last* has more than one meaning.

Pam's water will last through the game.

The word *last* in this sentence means Pam will have water until the end of the game.

Sam was last in line in the cafeteria.

The word *last* in this sentence means Sam was at the end of the line.

Rule Box

Reading the words and sentences around a word can help you choose the correct meaning of a multiple-meaning word.

Your Turn

Work with a partner.
Take turns.

Read each sentence.
Choose the correct meaning
for the underlined word.

1. That <u>kind</u> of bird is very rare.
   a. a type of something
   b. nice

2. Sue <u>lost</u> the contest.
   a. did not win
   b. no longer had

3. I saw the <u>bat</u> fly through the trees.
   a. an animal that can be seen at night
   b. an object used to hit a ball

4. The feather is <u>light</u>.
   a. not weighing much
   b. an electric device

Writing

Informational Writing

Sometimes, authors write to explain or tell about things. This kind of writing is called **informational writing.**

Long ago, people ate ice cream from a dish. Then, two men invented the ice cream cone.

Your Turn

Look at the pictures. Which sentences give information about the pictures?

1. I like to practice writing with a pencil.

2. I like to play outside on sunny days.

3. I get information from my computer.
   I write the information on a notepad.

4. My teacher helps me with writing.

Write a Nonfiction Story

You have read about how things change through inventions.

What do you think is a good invention? Mike wrote about airplanes.

I think a good invention is the airplane. People always wanted to fly. They invented many planes, but not all of them worked!

Now we can travel very fast on a plane.

SPELLING

The letters *ee* and *ea* can stand for the long *e* sound as in **feet** and **seat**.

Write!

Think about another good invention. What is it? What did people do in the past, when it didn't exist? Write about it.

The Big Question

How is life today different than it was a long time ago?

Written

Write about School

What was school like in the past? What is school like today?

Oral

Interview an Adult

Ask an adult what school was like when they were your age. What did they learn? How did they learn?

Visual/Active

Teach How

Ask an adult to tell you about a game he or she used to play. Teach a partner how to play that game. Then play the game together.

Unit 5

Plants and Animals

Plants and animals
are living things.
They are important
in our world.

?

The Big Question
Why are plants and
animals important
in our world?

Let's Talk

Tell about plants and
animals where you live.
Which ones do you like?

What Do You Know about Plants and Animals?

Some animals help us.

We can use some plants as food.

We need animals and plants so we can live.

We can take care of plants.

We can take care of animals.

Your Turn

What is your favorite animal? Why? Tell about it.

Sing about Plants and Animals

In Our World

Cats and birds and fish and dogs,
they are animals in our world.
Fleas and flies, elephants, too,
whales and turtles and kangaroos,
cats and birds and fish and dogs,
they are animals in our world.

Daisies, roses, and palm trees —
plants that make our planet green.
Bushes of blueberries, and lemon trees,
pines and ferns and strawberries,
daisies, roses, and palm trees —
plants that make our planet green.

197

What Lives in a Tree

Vocabulary

Words to Know

I **have** a **small** ball. I **found** the ball at the beach.

The **squirrel** **nibbles** on a nut.

It's **delicious**!

Your Turn

Pick one word from either box.
Use the word in a sentence.

198

Phonics

Long o; soft g

Look at each picture. Read the word.

soap

gem

snow

cold

Your Turn

Point to the word that names the picture. Read the word.

boat   bite

gull   goal

stop   stage

got   goat

About the Story

Who is in the story?

bird   **spider**   **squirrel**

Where does the story happen?

The story happens in trees.

What Lives in a Tree?

by Sonia Black

A nest with eggs sits high in this tree.
Twigs, twine, and trash make up this
nest. Mother bird will wait till her chicks
grow in the eggs. Small chicks will poke
holes and crack the shells. Then, Mother
will find a meal her chicks can eat.

A spider spins a sticky web high in an oak tree. When it has finished, it will hide and wait for an insect. An insect will fly by and get stuck in the web. Then our spider pal can have a fine meal to eat.

Some squirrels roam around and make homes in trees. They hunt and find nuts that lie on the ground. They crack nuts with sharp teeth.

This squirrel nibbles on a tasty snack. He eats his nut on a soft leaf pile.

Squirrels jump from homes in trees and try to find a lot of nuts. They dig in leaf piles to find nuts. They find loads and loads of nuts and pile them up at home. They keep the nuts at home to eat when it is cold outside.

We don't live in trees. But trees provide things we need to live.

We get small foods like nuts and berries from trees. Books that kids read are made from trees. A tree gave us this book.

Trees help clean our air. Trees help us have the clean air we need to breathe.

And trees can make the homes we go to each night.

Think It Over

1. Who makes a nest in the tree?

2. What will get stuck in the spider's web?

3. What do squirrels eat?

4. What can we get from trees?

Trees

Bloom ▶

This is a cherry tree in full bloom. In the summer, people will pick red cherries.

◀ **Ripe**

Soon, someone will pick this ripe peach.

Furniture ▶

This tree is called a sycamore maple. People make furniture from this kind of tree.

▲ **Almond**

Almonds grow on this tree.

Activity to Do!

These two pages tell about how trees help people.

- Think of a few other ways people use trees.
- Find pictures that show other ways trees are used.
- Share your pictures with the class.

209

Sue the Tadpole

Sight Words

said

her

soon

water

Story Words

arms

shore

sign

Vocabulary

Words to Know

Mom was sitting with me. I **said** to **her**, "Let's go to the park **soon**. It's a sunny day!"

Mom said, "Let's take **water** and some healthy snacks to eat."

You have to have strong **arms** to row a boat!

We like to stay close to **shore**.

The **sign** is pointing straight ahead to the panda bear exhibit.

Your Turn

Pick one word from either box.

Use the word in a sentence.

Phonics

Letters: ew, ou

Look at the pictures. Read the words.

soup

screw

new

Phonics

moon

Your Turn

Name the pictures. Which words have the same sound
as the *ew* in **new**?

About the Story

Who is in the story?

Sue

Dad

Mom

Where does the story happen?

The story happens in a pond.

Sue the Tadpole

by Quentin Shue

illustrated by Kevin Rechin

Sue, the new tadpole, rests on a leaf.
She rests on a leaf in the deep blue water.
Dad and Mom see Sue. The bugs see Sue.
A fish sees Sue. A bird flies by. Sue feels
alone. Sue feels a bit scared.

Mom holds Sue. Sue is cold and
wet. She moans, "Mom, when will I be
a big frog?"

Mom says, "Soon. It is true. You will
be a big frog in a few weeks."

Sue swims in the pond. She is still
sad. She says, "I have no arms or legs. I
can dive. I can swim. But I cannot jump.
I want to be a real frog."

Sue sees Dad jump and hop. Dad
jumps from leaf to leaf. Sue is still sad.

"When will I grow to be a real frog?"
she asks.

"Soon," Dad says. "You will be a big
frog in a few weeks."

Sue is getting bigger. She has a tail.
But where are her arms and legs? A
fish swims by. The fish stops to chat
with Sue.

Sue is tired. She moans, "I have a tail
now, but I have no arms or legs. I want
to be a real frog." Sue wishes for arms
and legs so she can jump like her dad.

Time goes by. Sue swims in the deep blue water. Her legs are growing. She can swim faster now. She can't wait until she is big enough to swim with her dad.

Time goes by. Sue's legs grow and grow. New arms are growing, too. Sue can't wait until she can jump just like her dad.

Sue is excited. She says to Dad,
"Look at me. I can jump. I can hop.
Mom said I would get big. She said I
would grow. Mom was right, and I am
glad! Yippee!"

Dad and Sue sit on a lily pad. They
see their faces in the deep blue water. Sue
and Dad smile. They are so happy. Sue
is a real frog now. She can hop, and she
can jump. Sue wants to hop and jump
all the time.

Sue reads a sign on the shore. There is a jumping show.

Sue is a good jumper now. She wins the show. Sue gets a prize. Sue thinks, "Waiting for arms and legs was hard, but they were worth waiting for!"

Think It Over

1. Who is Sue?

2. What problem does Sue have?

3. How do Mom and Dad help Sue?

4. What happens to Sue at the end of the story?

Wild Cats

Vocabulary

Words to Know

We **always** wait in line to drink **more** water. We **never** take a long time drinking.

Birds and dogs are **animals**.

A **lion** is a male, and a **lioness** is a female.

A lion can be an **enemy** to smaller animals.

Sight Words

always

more

never

animals

Story Words

lion

lioness

enemy

Your Turn

Pick one word from either box.

Use the word in a sentence.

Phonics

Letters: *ow, ou*

Look at each picture. Read the word.

loud

town

Your Turn

Which letters stand for the missing sound?

_ _ l

cl _ _ d

cr _ _ n

m _ _ se

About the Story

Who is in the story?

lion

lioness

cub

Where does the story happen?

The story happens in Africa.

Wild Cats

by Leo Wilde

Many kinds of wild animals make homes in Africa. One kind is the big, strong, and proud type of cat named a lion. A female cat is a lioness. A bigger male cat is a lion. A long mane grows on his thick neck and wide shoulders. These cats have tan, brown, and orange fur. It is sleek and shiny.

This little cat is a cub. The big cats are his mom and dad. Lion cubs have spots when they are just born. Can you still see spots on this little cub, now? As cubs grow up, their spots fade out.

Lions prowl in wide, open grasslands. This is their home, or habitat.

It can be cool and wet in the grasslands. It can also be dry in the grasslands. Big cats can make a home in wet or dry grasslands.

Lions always hunt animals to get a meal. Female lions hunt more than males. A lioness might get tired from a hunt. Then she needs sleep, so cubs spend time with Dad. This cub likes to pat Dad's mane and growl softly. Mom and Dad will teach the cub how to hunt.

Most big cats hunt while it is night. When a hunt ends, it is time for a nap. Big cats lie on the ground and rest. In fact, big cats can lie down and nap all day long! They rest to save energy. Big cats will hunt again when they wake up.

 Oral	Visual/Active
Introduce a Plant or an Animal	**Draw Your Favorite Plant or Animal**
Tell the class about a plant or an animal from another country.	Draw a picture of your favorite plant or animal.

Places Around the World

People live in different parts of the world. They have different cultures and languages.

Let's Talk

Tell about other countries you know. What language do people speak there?

What Do You Know about Places Around the World?

In some countries, brides wear a red dress.

In some countries, brides wear a white dress.

Some people use chopsticks to eat.

In parts of the world, people use forks and knives to eat.

Some people do not use cars to travel. They travel by camel.

Your Turn

Have you seen more pictures of people in other countries? How were they different from you? Tell about it.

247

Sing about Places Around the World

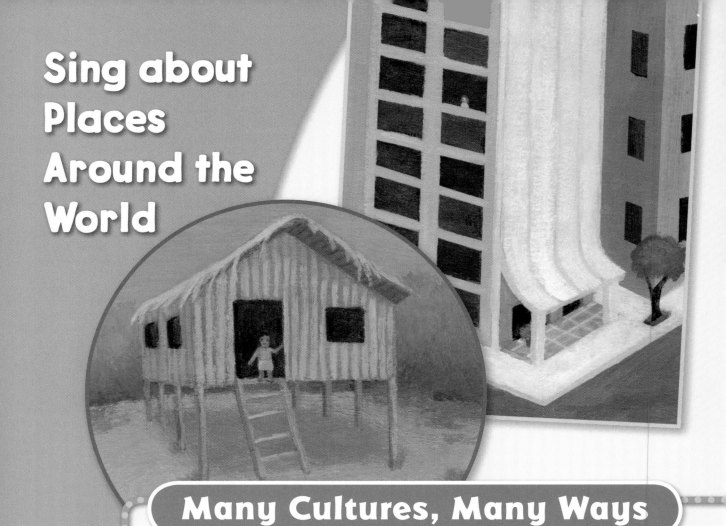

Many Cultures, Many Ways

All around the world,

   people come and go.

They live in little houses,

   tall buildings, farms, and more.

They dress in thick, warm coats,

   in turbans, and light shirts.

There are many, many cultures,

   and many, many ways.

Some kids walk to school,
  some kids go by car.
Others go by bike,
  or on a camel's back.
They all will study hard,
  and soon they will learn
  there are many, many countries,
  and many, many ways.

Pen Pals

Vocabulary

Words to Know

We want to go **around** the **world** to a **warm** place!

There are many kinds of **vegetables**

A **cabbage** is a vegetable.

Eating **tofu** is good for you. It gives you energy!

Your Turn

Pick one word from either box.

Use the word in a sentence.

Phonics

R controlled vowels: *ir, er, ur*

Look at each picture. Read the word.

girl

sunburn

winter

shirt

Phonics

bird

nurse

fern

Your Turn

Point to the word that names the picture.

Read the word.

bed   bird

skirt   skit

cold   curl

summer   smell

251

About the Story

Who is in the story?

Bayo   **Lee**   **Tori**

Where does the story happen?

Nigeria   **Ireland**   **Japan**

Pen Pals

by Jeff Cole

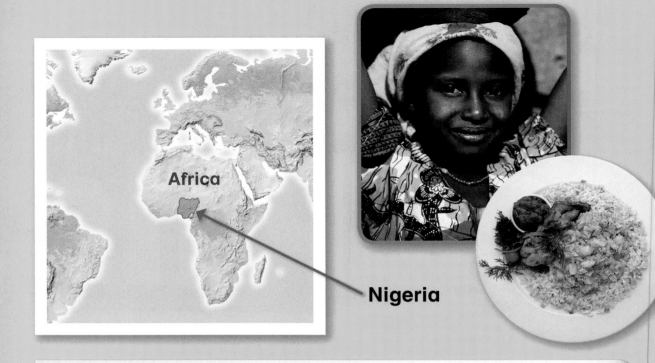

Africa

Nigeria

Dear Pen Pal,

My name is Bayo. My home is in Nigeria. It is hot and dry in my land.

I like to eat warm bread with meat and rice. Yams, soups, and stews are things I eat, too.

I like to play tag with my friends. I chase them, and I run as fast as I can.

I think we can make friends with each other. I hope you send me a note.

Bayo

Ireland

Europe

Dear Pen Pal,

    My name is Lee. Ireland is my home. It is not hot and dry. It is a bit wet.

    I like to eat a meal with cabbage and meat. Mom cooks in a big pot. I eat out of a bowl.

    My dog, Big Skip, and I can herd sheep. Big Skip can run and round up lost sheep.

    I want to find out about you and your world. It will be fun.

Lee

Asia

Japan

Dear Pen Pal,

My name is Tori. That name means bird in my land, Japan.

I like to eat vegetables, tofu, fish, and rice. On warm days, I like to fly my big, red kite. It is fun.

I hope you send a note. First I will read it. Then I will send a note back.

I want to know about your world. We can be pen pals.

Tori

Think It Over

1. Where does Bayo live?

2. What job does Big Skip have?

3. Do you like to eat what Tori eats? Why or why not?

4. Why do these children eat such different foods?

Vocabulary

Words to Know

It's Monday **morning**. **Once** I wake up, I will eat breakfast.

We **work** hard in **school**!

Let's look at this map for a **moment**. What **different** countries do you see?

This is Greenland. It is part of a **country** called Denmark.

Your Turn

Pick one word from either box.

Use the word in a sentence.

Phonics

R controlled vowel: *ar*

Look at each picture. Read the word.

stars

park

jar

shark

Your Turn

Name the pictures.

Which words have the same sound as the *ar* in *card*?

259

About the Story

Who is in the story?

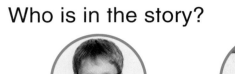

Mark

Star

Carl

Jane

Ned

Dar

Where and at what time does this story happen?

Berlin, Germany
4:00 P.M.

Hong Kong, China
11:00 P.M.

Denver, United States
8:00 A.M.

New Delhi, India
8:30 P.M.

Buenos Aires, Argentina
Noon

Nairobi, Kenya
6:00 P.M.

Time at School and at Home

by Sam Page

My name is Mark.

This morning I will find out about kids from different lands. I will use this globe. This globe will show where kids live.

I will read a book. I will read about kids in other lands. It will be fun to work and find out new facts.

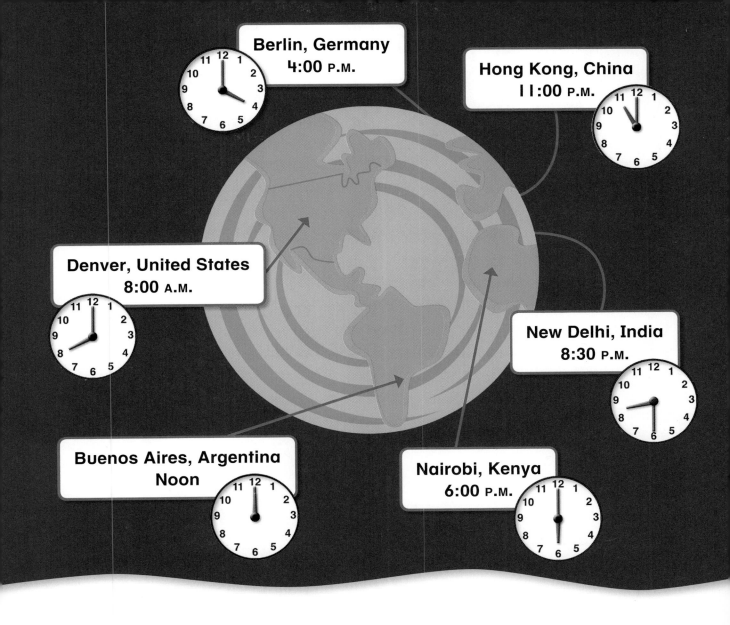

Green means *land* on this globe. **Blue** means *water*.

I will send a note to girls and boys in each country. I will ask them to tell me lots of things. I can ask how girls and boys go to school. I can learn what games they play.

Denver, Colorado, USA
8:00 A.M.

This is Star. In the morning, Star rides a bus to school. Star likes to share a seat with her best friend.

Buenos Aires, Argentina
Noon

This is Carl. Carl likes to eat lunch with his friends. Carl has fun in each moment of the day.

Berlin, Germany
4:00 P.M.

This is Jane and her dad. After school, Jane and her dad visit a big park. They will go home when it gets dark.

Nairobi, Kenya
6:00 P.M.

These boys like to play soccer after school. Once the boys won a big game. Today, Jim, Sam, and Ned will play and then go home to eat.

New Delhi, India
8:30 P.M.

This is Hana. Hana will do her work when she gets home. Once Hana is done, she will rest.

Hong Kong, China
11:00 P.M.

This is Dar. Dar has had a long day. He likes to work hard. He had fun at school. He had fun at home. Now it is time for sleep.

Think It Over

1. What does Mark want to find out?

2. What does green mean on Mark's globe?

3. How does Star go to school?

4. Would you like to visit any of the places you read about? Why?

Vocabulary

Words to Know

It's raining! It **would** be **better** to wait before I go outside.

Sight Words

would

better

only

under

Only two kids fit **under** this umbrella.

Story Words

students

continent

The third-grade **students** in my school study geography.

We live on the **continent** of North America.

Your Turn

Pick one word from either box.

Use the word in a sentence.

Phonics

R controlled vowels: *or*, *ore*

Look at each picture. Read the word.

storm

fork

shore

Phonics

horn

store

Your Turn

Name the pictures.

Which words have the same sound as the *or* in **horn**?

About the Story

What is this story about?

schools

Where does this story happen?

The story happens around the world.

Schools Around the World

You are here.

by Skip Flag

This class would like to learn more about students around the world. Pictures and maps will help this class find out more.

This class can also read notes
from students in other lands.
They will like to get lots of letters
from kids in other lands.

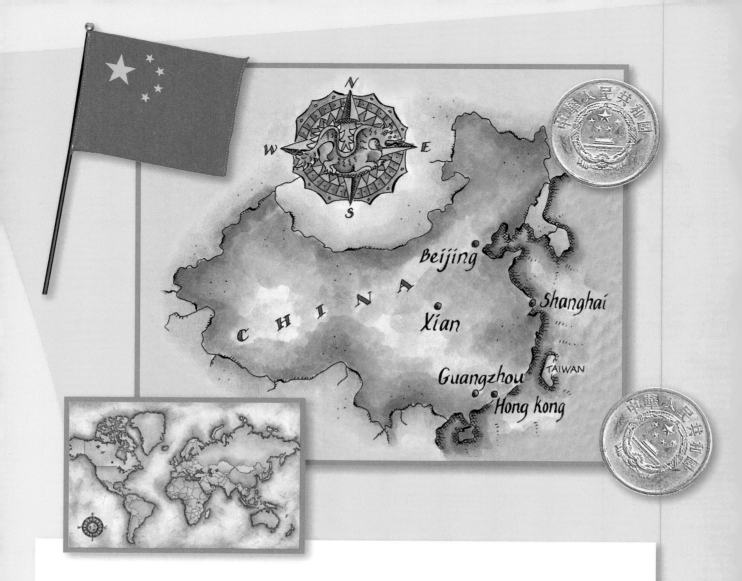

Dear Class,

I live on a big continent. It is called Asia. I live in a country called China. This map will show you where it is.

My flag is red with yellow stars on it. It has one big star. The other stars are not big. I would like to see your flag.

I want to be a better student. I work hard for my teacher. I stand up and read in class.

When it is time for lunch, I eat with girls and boys in my class. When I go home, I help my mom and dad. Then I go to sleep.

Chun

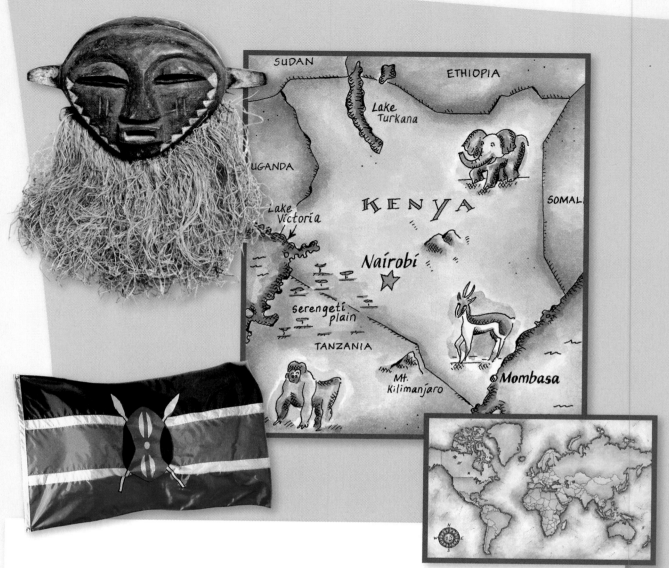

Dear Class,

I live in Kenya. This is my flag. It is black and red and green. It has white stripes.

It is hot in my land. My home is close to a big sea. When it is hot, I jump in the sea. I swim under big waves.

My school is lots of fun. I like to read and sing and dance in class. When it is time for lunch, I eat under a big tree in the yard.

At home, I have chores to do. I like my school work better than my chores.

Ande

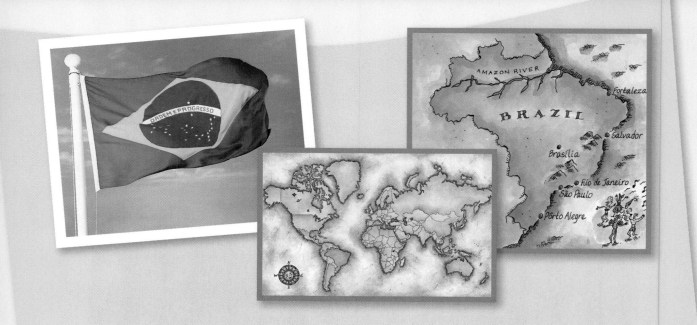

Dear Class,

    I was born in Brazil. This is my flag. Green is for land and blue is for sea. Yellow is for a big sun that shines each day. The sun helps palm trees grow in my land.

    My home is by the shore. I play in warm sand.

    I would like to learn more about your land. Please send notes back to help me learn.

Marco

Think It Over

1. Where is Chun from?

2. Where does Ande live?

3. Where is Marco's home?

4. Which school would you like to visit? Why?

School Children Around the World

◀ **Chicago**
These students go to school in Chicago, Illinois, USA.

South Africa ▶
Former President Clinton meets school children in South Africa.

Russia ▶
These Russian
school children
walk to school
through the snow.

▲ **China**
Some Chinese school
children wear uniforms
like the ones shown here.

Activity to Do!

These two pages use pictures and
words to tell about school children
around the world.

- Think about how school children
  from around the world are alike.
  How are they different?
- Find pictures that show other
  school children.
- Share your pictures with the class.

281

Word Analysis

Suffixes

A **suffix** is a word part added to the end of a word. A suffix changes the meaning of the word. Suffixes can help you understand new words.

> rainy = rain + y   slowly = slow + ly

Rule Box

The suffix *y* means "full of." So **rainy** means "full of rain."

The suffix *ly* means "in a certain way." So **slowly** means "to be slow."

Your Turn

Work with a partner.
Take turns.

- Read each pair of sentences.

- Say the underlined word aloud.

- Add a suffix to the underlined word to complete the second sentence.

1. The beach is full of <u>sand</u>.
   The beach is ___.

2. The dog moved in a <u>quick</u> way.
   The dog moved ___.

3. The grass looked clean and <u>fresh</u>.
   The grass was ___ cut.

Writing

Narrative Writing

Authors often write to tell a story about what they saw or did. This kind of writing is called **narrative writing.**

I remember the first time I played soccer. My good friend was on my team. We won our first game, and we were so happy. It was a great day!

Your Turn

Read each sentence. Tell what the person saw or did.

1. I tried out for the soccer team.

2. My dad and I saw a ball in the store.

3. We can play soccer in the park.

4. I saw my brother's team win.

Write a Narrative Paragraph

You have read about schools around the world.

Ted wrote about his friends in school.

I have good friends in school. When we have tests, we study together. We help one another with our homework, too. Our teachers are nice and give us extra help when we do not understand. I think my school is the best.

SPELLING

When the letters *wr* appear at the beginning of a word, the *w* is silent.

wrist   wrap

Write!

What do you remember about this year at school? What did you like doing?

Write about it.

Unit 6 Wrap Up

The Big Question

How are countries alike and different?

Written

Write about a Favorite Country

Write about a country you would like to visit. Include details that make this country special to you.

Oral

Introduce your Favorite Country

Tell the class about your favorite country. Explain what is special about it.

 ## Visual/Active

Draw a Favorite Country

Draw a country you have been to or one you would like to visit. Include special sites from that country. Share your drawing with the class.

Picture Dictionary

ago ▶ ball

A

ago

Long **ago** we washed clothes by hand.

always

We **always** wait in line.

animals

Lions are **animals**.

apartment

An **apartment** is a place to live.

are

We **are** on a team.

arms

I have two **arms**.

around

My belt goes **around** my waist.

B

baby

A **baby** is small.

ball

The girl runs with the **ball**.

baseball

I play **baseball**.

beach

The **beach** is by the sea.

beautiful

A rainbow is **beautiful**.

beehive

Bees live in a **beehive**.

better

Television is **better** today than it was long ago.

big

The box is **big**.

board

The teacher wrote on the **board**.

but

It is hard, **but** Jack can climb high.

A
B
C
D
E
F
G
H
I
J
K
L
M
N
O
P
Q
R
S
T
U
V
W
X
Y
Z

buy

Gramps and Dan **buy** food.

by

The swan swims **by** the people.

─── C ───

cabbage

Cabbage is a green vegetable.

children

The **children** built a sand castle.

chore

I make my bed. I do a **chore**.

clean

I will **clean** the desk.

coat

I wear a **coat** and a hat.

cold

It is **cold** outside.

continent

A **continent** is a big area of land.

country

Spain is a **country**.

D

day

I go out in the **day**.

delicious

Chicken is a **delicious** food.

different

Blue is **different** from red.

does

Does Jed live in an apartment?

done

We rest when we are **done** playing.

down

Dad puts the ball **down**.

dry

The clothes will **dry** on the line.

eat

We **eat** dinner.

e-mail

I will send you an **e-mail**.

enemy

The shark is the **enemy** of the fish.

F

family

This is my **family**.

feels

The dog **feels** wet.

five

There are **five** people.

football

We play **football**.

for

The coat is **for** him.

found

The squirrel **found** a nut.

friends

Friends play games together.

funny

Jen wore a **funny** hat.

G

give

Give the baby a bottle.

good

Ice cream tastes **good**.

grown-up

My dad is a **grown-up**.

H

have

I **have** a ball.

her

Her clothes are clean.

hold

I **hold** the ball.

horse

Jen rides on a **horse**.

A
B
C
D
E
F
G
H
I
J
K
L
M
N
O
P
Q
R
S
T
U
V
W
X
Y
Z

293

A
B
C
D
E
F
G
H
I
J
K
L
M
N
O
P
Q
R
S
T
U
V
W
X
Y
Z

house

I live in a **house**.

hurt

Now Mike will not get **hurt**.

I

ice

Ice is cold.

K

keep

My scarf will **keep** me warm.

L

laugh

I **laugh** with my family.

learn

I **learn** at school.

letter

The **letter** came in the mail.

light

The baby felt **light**.

lion

A **lion** roars.

lioness

A **lioness** is a female lion.

294

machine

machine
This **machine** has buttons.

middle

This man is in the **middle**.

moment

The candles stay lit for a **moment**.

more

The home team has **more** points.

morning

I wake up in the **morning**.

near

We stand **near** the truck.

never

We **never** talk when the teacher reads.

nibbles

The mouse **nibbles** on the cheese.

now

Now the swan is big.

A
B
C
D
E
F
G
H
I
J
K
L
M
N
O
P
Q
R
S
T
U
V
W
X
Y
Z

O

once

Once I finish my homework, I can play!

only

Only boys go to this school.

or

Choose a green **or** red **or** blue pen.

other

What **other** flavors do you like?

own

My parents **own** this house.

P

parents

Parents take care of you.

people

Many **people** had fun on the ride.

play

We **play** baseball.

puppy

A **puppy** is a small dog.

R

roads

We cross two **roads** every day.

roost

The hens like to **roost** in nests.

S

said

The girl **said**, "We can make this together."

school

I go to **school** to learn.

shore

It is fun to visit the **shore**.

sign

I can read this **sign**.

simple

Math can be **simple**.

sing

Gramps can **sing**.

small

Berries are **small** fruit.

A
B
C
D
E
F
G
H
I
J
K
L
M
N
O
P
Q
R
S
T
U
V
W
X
Y
Z

A
B
C
D
E
F
G
H
I
J
K
L
M
N
O
P
Q
R
S
T
U
V
W
X
Y
Z

snow

Snow falls when it is cold.

soccer

He plays **soccer**.

some

Some of the eggs are missing.

soon

I hope the rain stops **soon**.

special

Thanksgiving is a **special** day.

squirrel

The **squirrel** has a big tail.

students

Students are in a class.

sure

I am **sure** this is a cherry tree.

swans

Swans are white.

298

T

tasty

Chocolate is a **tasty** treat.

today

Today we wash clothes in a machine, not by hand.

tofu

Tofu is a healthy snack.

trailer

We live in a **trailer**.

treat

A cookie is a **treat**.

tree

A **tree** can grow tall.

U

under

They sit **under** the umbrella.

V

vegetables

Vegetables are good to eat.

A B C D E F G H I J K L M N O P Q R S T U V W X Y Z

very

I can throw **very** high.

W

waffle

A **waffle** is tasty.

warm

The children are **warm** in their coats and hats.

was

The girl **was** singing.

wash

I **wash** my hands.

washboard

A **washboard** was used to wash clothes long ago.

water

The boat is on the **water**.

we

We are a family.

A B C D E F G H I J K L M N O P Q R S T U V W X Y Z

were

All people **were** small at first.

who

Who is holding the flowers?

work

We **work** hard in school.

would

I **would** like to dance.

year

Twelve months make a **year**.

yellow

He has a **yellow** house.

A
B
C
D
E
F
G
H
I
J
K
L
M
N
O
P
Q
R
S
T
U
V
W
X
Y
Z

Credits